FORT RINELLA
AND ITS ARMSTRONG
100-TON GUN
Kalkara

MARIO FARRUGIA

HERITAGE BOOKS
FOR FONDAZZJONI WIRT ARTNA
2004

Acknowledgements

Primary acknowledgements for the historical content of this book are due to Major Denis Rollo, RA, a former gunner officer and a much-acclaimed authority on Royal Artillery history and to David Moore, treasurer of the Palmerston Forts Society and a keen student of Victorian artillery and fortifications. My personal debt goes towards my unfailing friend, Duncan S. Williams, also of the Palmerston Forts Society and fellow gunner re-enactor, for his good advice and kind assistance received on my frequent study trips to the UK.

In this sense I am also indebted towards the staff of the Public Record Office, Kew; the Royal Artillery Historical Library, Woolwich; the National Artillery Museum at Fort Nelson, Portsmouth; the Royal Engineers Library at Chatham; and the Ufficcio Storico della Marina, Rome. Recognition is due to Dr Stanley Zammit, MD who during his tenure of the environment portfolio as parliamentary secretary was solely instrumental in seeing Rinella Battery entrusted to the care of Fondazzjoni Wirt Artna. I am thankful to Ian Ellis for allowing me to use some of his precious historic photographs from the famous Ellis photographic collection, Kevin Cassar for proof-reading the text; and to Stephen C. Spiteri, Ray Cachia Zammit and Louis J. Scerri for their support.

Finally, my gratitude as a Maltese citizen goes to those volunteers from *Fondazzjoni Wirt Artna*, who out of their own free will have contributed time and energy in restoring this unique piece of history back to its former state: Alfred and David Bonello, Steve Borg, Stefan Camilleri, Kevin Cassar, Ramon Corrado, Denis Darmanin, Neville Ebejer, John Hili, Godwin Hampton, Alan Lloyd, Joseph Magro Conti, Ray and Randolph Mamo, and Jeffery Scibberas. To them this book is dedicated.

Insight Heritage Guides Series No: 1
General Editor: Louis J. Scerri

Published by Heritage Books, a subsidiary of Midsea Books Ltd, for Fondazzjoni Wirt Artna – Malta Heritage Trust, Notre Dame Gate, St Edward's Road, Vittoriosa

First published in 2002. This edition 2004.

Insight Heritage Guides is a series of books intended to give an insight into aspects and sites of Malta's rich heritage, culture and traditions.

Produced by Mizzi Design & Graphic Services
Printed by Gutenberg Press

ISBN: 99932-39-05-4

Photo Credits

The publisher and author would like to thank the following organizations and individuals for the reproduction of photos in this publication.

Ufficcio Storico della Marina Militare, Italy
Public Record Office, UK
Illustrated London News
Fondazzjoni Wirt Artna
Royal Engineers Library, Chatham, UK
Tito Vallejo
Elmy Bretney, Dexter
War Museum Association, Malta
Royal Artillery Historical Trust, UK
Virtù Steamship Co. Ltd.
Navy and Army Illustrated
War Office Library, UK
Gibraltar Museum

Introduction

Rinella Battery was built in the late nineteenth century at a time when the growing naval power of nearby Italy posed a potential threat to British commerce and navigation in the Mediterranean.

After the serious defeats suffered at the hands of the Austrians at Custozza and Lissa in 1866, in 1873 Italy gave start to the rebuilding of its naval and military forces. In reforming their navy, the Italians decided to part with the conventional concept of a fleet based on numerous vessels armed with a whole array of armament. Instead, they aimed at a small ironclad fleet formed from large and powerful ships, armed in turn with a limited number of heavy cannon.

This situation caused the British much warranted concern, for the Italians could disrupt British commerce in the Mediterranean, something which could have severe repercussions not just on British trade but also on the effective running of the Empire itself. This led Britain to hurriedly strengthen the coast defences of Malta and Gibraltar and also to commission a new ironclad armed with four 16-inch guns to rival any of the new Italian ships, both in strength and firepower – HMS *Inflexible*. Four 100-ton gun batteries were provided at Gibraltar and Malta in an effort to secure the two important naval stations against the possibility of naval attack or blockade. Rinella Battery was thus built.

At the time of building, the 100-ton gun batteries were not only exorbitantly expensive but also highly innovative in their design. They were the first defence structures in history to employ a mechanical system that was totally independent of human power for the working and loading of their monstrous armament. On the other hand, the 100-ton gun went down in history as the epitome of muzzle-loading technology. Its building was long and expensive, and required the world's largest equipment in terms of a steam hammer to forge it and cranes to lift it. Yet, in its day, it was a veritable wonder of science and engineering that was unparalleled not just in size but also in its devastating performance. In practice the 100-ton gun proved to be nothing but a seven-day wonder, as it was soon eclipsed by newer technology that came into use at around the same time of its entry into service.

Today, after more than a century in disuse, both gun and battery are back in the limelight. Indeed, they no longer serve as a deterrent against enemy blockade or attack. Rather, they now represent a unique window on a not too distant age of empire when the force of arms was not simply a matter of national security or pride, but also a much-prized weapon in the complex arsenal of diplomacy. Through the unstinting and selfless effort of volunteer members of Fondazzjoni Wirt Artna both battery and gun were secured for posterity. They are today open to visiting as well deserved monuments to a time in history when the dependence of man on machine became increasingly a daily fact of life.

Mario Farrugia

The Battle of Lissa and the great Italian naval crisis

The Armstrong 100-ton gun and Rinella Battery itself, owe their origins to a most unfortunate chapter in Italian naval history. In 1866, newly-unified Italy entered into alliance with Prussia with high hopes of finally reducing its traditional foe, Austria. On 20 July 1866, Italy's full naval might, comprising the combined navies of the former Sardinian and Neapolitan kingdoms, went into battle against a much smaller Austrian navy close to the island of Lissa in the Adriatic. There, Italy's naval prestige was put to test against that of Austria, in what was to become history's only naval battle between fleets of steam-powered ironclads.

The tragic ramming of the *Re d'Italia* during the Battle of Lissa, 1866

For the Italians, this battle carried high hopes and great significance, as it gave them their first opportunity to face Austria as a unified nation. It also offered them the unique chance, at an advantage of four to one, to avenge the severe blow received on land at Custozza, just weeks before. But this was not to be, for in a matter of minutes their superior forces were routed and dispersed in disgraceful disarray by the sheer dare of Austrian initiative who, against heavy odds, managed to turn what seemed to the world as certain defeat into a decisive victory.

This unexpected defeat brought with it much resentment amongst all classes of Italian society against their navy, to the extent that even King Victor Emmanuel II himself saw fit to prohibit any naval officers from serving on his staff or to accompany him on official business.

The first ironclad engagement in history took place between the USS *Monitor* and the CSS *Merrimac* during the American Civil War, 1860

A long period of soul-searching ensued during which it was even contemplated to make away with the naval service altogether. But after a while, common sense prevailed. Italy with probably the longest coast to defend in the whole of Europe could not do without the protection of an effective navy. This finally led, in 1873, Admiral Augusto Riboty, Minister for the Navy, to declare in parliament his government's intentions to bring an end to this long protracted crisis by rebuilding the navy anew into a veritable fighting force equipped with the most powerful ships possible.

For the rebuilding of their naval forces, the Italians engaged Admiral Benedetto Brin as *Ispettore del Genio Navale*. Brin was himself a first-rate naval authority. During the American Civil War he had gained important first-hand experience in ironclad design and building following a stint in that conflict. He was later to use this experience in reforming the Italian naval service by offering it new

ironclads based on the American monitor system, yet far superior in every respect. His new battleships were also to be armed with the largest guns possible – the 100-ton gun.

From the Monitor to the Duilio – the new Italian ironclad navy

The basis of the new navy was to be a new breed of warship based on the combined lessons learnt in

Top: Benedetto Brin, Chief Constructor of the Italian navy, 1833-98

Bottom: Elevation and plan of the Italian battleship, *Duilio*

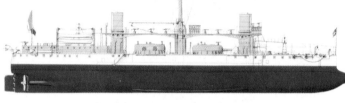

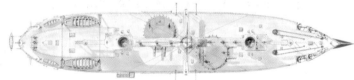

Top: Construction of the *Duilio* at Castellamare di Stabbia, Naples. Note the large opening in the side for the thick armour plate

Centre: Section of the *Duilio* showing loading arrangements for the 100-ton guns on board

The *Duilio* – class battleships had a displacement of 12,071 tons, a maximum speed of 15 knots, and were each armed with four 100-ton guns emplaced in pairs, in two circular turrets, placed off the centre line, to allow axial fire forward and aft. They were also equipped with a submerged torpedo tube in the bow. The *Duilio* alone was provided with an on-board torpedo boat that could be launched to act independently or to assist in the defence of the ship against the threat from similar boats. The two ships were protected by an unprecedented 22 inches of steel armour and were fitted with a strong ram at their bow following the conclusions drawn from the Battle of Lissa.

the American Civil War and later at Lissa. During the American Civil War, lack of resources and adequate ship-building facilities led the Union navy to produce its own ironclads. One of these was the USS *Monitor* – a low freeboard vessel, covered in iron and armed with two 11-inch Dahlgren guns enclosed in a revolving turret that gave it all round fire. Although, the *Monitor* was hampered by numerous technical problems, the idea on which it was built was a great success.

A new concept in naval design evolved from the *Monitor*, that of combining the superior advantages of heavy armour with the speed of steam and the all round concentrated fire-power from few but heavy guns. The true modern battleship was thus born.

In 1873, contemporarily to Italy's *Decreto Legge* authorizing the reform of the navy, a new breed of Italian battleships was launched. In this class, two battleships were to be built, named after *Caio Duilio* – a Roman general and *Enrico Dandalo* – a medieval warrior captain respectively. Both ships were of near identical design.

Originally these ships were to be armed with four 35-ton guns. However, seeing the rapid way that the size of guns and ship-armour was increasing, Brin preferred to adopt the largest guns possible that would give the Italians a clear cut advantage on any other foreign ship afloat.

Italy had none of the industrial capacity to build such monstrous armament, so foreign assistance was sought. Sir William George Armstrong, the great English inventor, industrialist, and engineer from Newcastle, was approached to design and produce these monster guns for the Italians at his massive Elswick plant on the river Tyne. Armstrong who had a high sense of

FORT RINELLA AND ITS ARMSTRONG 100-TON GUN

enterprise was also at that time in the process of establishing a munitions plant at Pozzuoli in Italy.

Great Britain

Gibraltar Malta

Suez Canal

India

The British answer – HMS Inflexible

On their part, the British took great interest in the recent naval developments in Italy. Although no state of war existed between the two countries, Britain would not chance its free movement in the region. Neither would she compromise her tenure of Malta and Gibraltar, which served her as strategic coaling stations along the route to India through the recently-opened Suez Canal (1869). Her answer to this situation was the building of four coastal batteries in Malta and Gibraltar armed with the same type of ordnance as on board the Italian battleships. She also hastened to build a battleship

very similar to the Italian *Duilio* – the *Inflexible*.

The *Inflexible* was armed with four 16-inch RML 80-ton guns. These were produced by the Royal Gun Factory in Woolwich to rival the Armstrong gun. Nevertheless, they proved to be inferior to it in every respect. HMS *Inflexible* was designed by Nathaniel Barnaby, chief-constructor for

Map showing the 'Pink' route from Britain to India. The area marked in green is the extent of the British Empire c. 1900

HMS *Inflexible* – Britain's direct answer to Italy's *Duilio* in Malta's Grand harbour

heavily damaged. On her completion in October 1881, she was immediately sent to join the Mediterranean Fleet where she was to spend a good deal of her commissioned life based in Malta.

Development of the Armstrong 100-ton gun

The order for the first 100-ton gun was placed by the Italian government with Sir W.G. Armstrong & Co. in 1874. The first prototype was completed in 1876, when it was shipped for trials in Italy on board the Italian naval steamer *Europa*.

This occasion was not allowed to pass unnoticed for it was intentionally coupled with yet another important event in the history of the industrial development of Newcastle. In that same year, a new swing bridge had been completed by Armstrong to

Top: Illustration showing firing trials of the 80-ton gun produced by the Royal Gun Factory, Woolwich

Right: The 80-ton gun on its proof mount

Bottom: The inauguration of the Swing Bridge and the passage of the *Europa* Italian naval transport

the Royal Navy, and was launched in 1874. The *Inflexible* had a displacement of 11,880 tons, and a top speed of 14.7 knots. She was designed with a heavily-armoured (24 inches) iron citadel, capable of remaining afloat even if the unarmoured bow and stern were

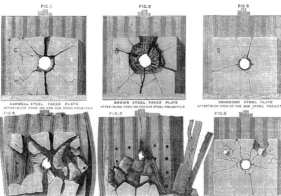

replace a much older structure, which restricted navigation up the river Tyne. Armstrong solved this problem with the design and construction of an ingenious hydraulic bridge that swung on its own axis to open the way for large vessels to proceed up river. At the time, this project was hailed as a great achievement, and one that opened new horizons for industrial progress in the area.

The arrival of the *Europa* transport at Elswick was made to coincide with the inauguration of the swing bridge. Although no official ceremonies were intended, the passage of this vessel past the bridge on its way to Armstrong's plant was conspicuously attended by Sir William G. Armstrong amid cannon fire, bands playing, and much bunting. George Rendel, Armstrong's loyal assistant and possible designer of the 100-ton gun, was also there. So were thousands of curious spectators who filled both sides of the banks of the river to be awed by yet another marvel of Armstrong's great engineering creations. The next day, the 100-ton gun was embarked on the *Europa* with the help of a huge hydraulic crane.

Top left: View of Elswick works along the banks of the Tyne, Newcastle

Left centre: Test proofing of the first 100-ton gun at La Spezia, Italy

Top right: Shattered iron and steel targets after being shot at by the 100-ton during the La Spezia trials

Below: Lord William George Armstrong of Craigside, 1810-1900

Left: Disembarking of first 100-ton gun at La Spezia using a 160-ton hydraulic crane designed by Armstrong. This crane is still extant at the Arsenale

Vittorio Emmanele II, first King of unified Italy 1820-78

Right: George Rendel, Armstrong's dedicated companion and likely creator of the 100-ton gun

On reaching La Spezia in Italy, the 100-ton gun went through rigorous testing by the Italian navy. A much-publicized event was held for which delegates from different countries were invited. The gun was mounted on a floating pontoon in a small man-made harbour complete with a breakwater to guard as much as possible against the disturbances of the sea, which could derange the experiments with the gun.

The gun was fired against iron targets set a good distance away on land. But after a while all experiments were temporarily suspended. It was found that the scale of devastation caused by this gun did not only result in the smashing of all the targets hit but it also effected all others in the vicinity. Although incomplete, from these experiments it was concluded that the calibre of this piece was to be increased by a $^3/_4$ inch from the original 17 inches. Its chamber was also to be increased to receive a charge of 450 lbs. as against the initial one of 370 lbs. used throughout these trials.

King Victor Emmanuel II of Italy was so moved by the impressive results obtained during these experiments that he immediately conferred the distinction of Grand Officer of the United Orders of St Maurice and St Lazarus on William Armstrong. He also made George Rendel and Captain Andrew Noble commanders of the Order of the Crown of Italy for the considerably part they played in the design and development of this monstrous piece.

Subsequently, more trials were held in Italy with the 100-ton gun, but there was no doubt from the very start that this was to be the wonder weapon around which Italy's unfortunate if not disgraced navy was to rise like a phoenix.

As one can imagine, Britain kept a very close eye on these trials. The stunning results achieved throughout, left her no choice other than to start her own monster gun programme. This resulted in the ill-fated 80-ton rifled muzzle-loading 16-inch gun of

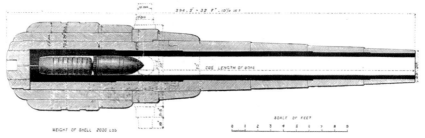

which only six were to be made. Four of these guns were built as main armament for HMS *Inflexible*. Another two of these guns were mounted on land in an armoured turret to protect the admiralty pier at Dover as part of the same drive to arm Malta and Gibraltar with 100-ton guns.

The 80-ton gun was in many ways inferior to Armstrong's *armour-puncher* as the press now daubed the new 100-ton gun. This would eventually lead the British government to obtain from Armstrong four of these guns for the arming of Malta and Gibraltar.

Section showing construction of 100-ton gun barrel

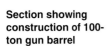

WEIGHT OF SHELL 2000 LBS

SCALE OF FEET

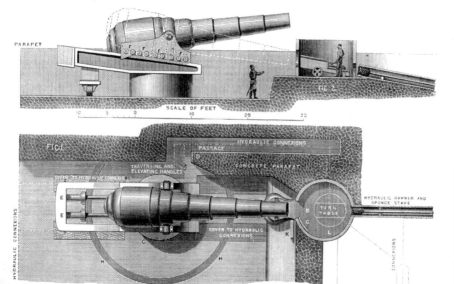

```
10    5    0
         10         20              30
```

Detail of practice battery as built at Shoeburyness proving grounds to test loading arrangements for the 100-ton gun using steam generated hydraulic power

Technical description of the 100-ton gun

The 100-ton gun was designed and built according to Armstrong's patented method of gun manufacture. This system consisted mainly of a built-up barrel using different wrought iron tubes shrunken one over the other to form a compact jacket over a rifled steel bore. This system was based on an accurate scientific calculation that established the exact points of stress occurring in a gun when fired. Using this data, Armstrong would distribute the thickness of metal in a barrel where it was most needed, which in most cases resulted in odd bottle shaped guns.

The final version of the 100-ton gun weighed 102 tons. Its barrel was formed from 28 different tubes. It had 21 projections forming its rifling. The calibre was 17.72 inches and it could fire a one-ton shell up to some eight miles. Within a 3-mile range it could penetrate 15 inches of wrought iron

armour that increased at close range. As propellant it used 450 lbs. of prismatic black powder which, along with the shell, brought the cost of each round to an astronomic £100!

The gun was mounted on a carriage and slide. The carriage was fitted at its back with two recoil cylinders to absorb the violent recoil generated by the gun when fired.

Traversing, loading, and depressing of this piece was all done mechanically using steam-driven hydraulic power that reduced crew numbers to a mere handful. Using this system this gun could fire once every 20 minutes onboard the Italian ships and every 6 minutes on land. The resulting discrepancy between loading on land and sea stood mainly in the major difficulty that loading on board represented. In fact, whilst on land the gun would be loaded at one go using a 60-foot long hydraulic rammer. On board the Italian ships it could only be loaded in stages owing to restriction of space.

The gun could be fired by using either a lanyard drawn friction tube or

Record Plans of Fort Rinella

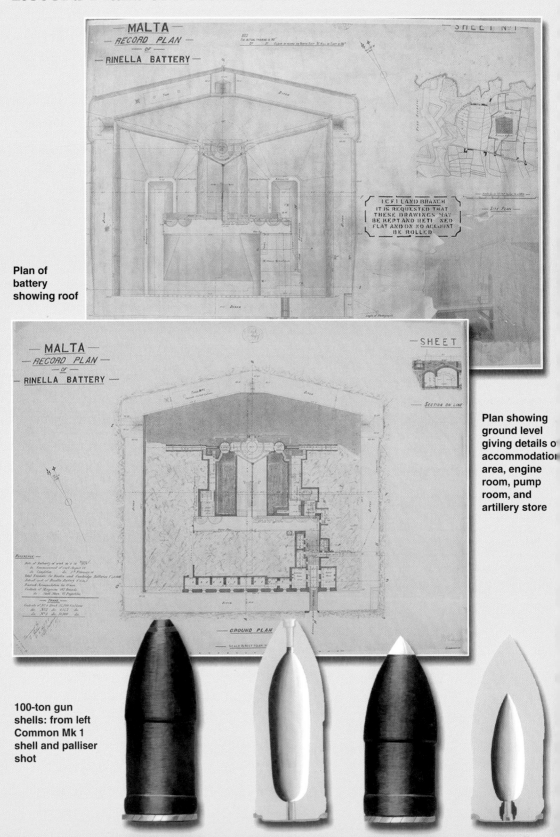

Plan of battery showing roof

Plan showing ground level giving details of accommodation area, engine room, pump room, and artillery store

100-ton gun shells: from left Common Mk 1 shell and palliser shot

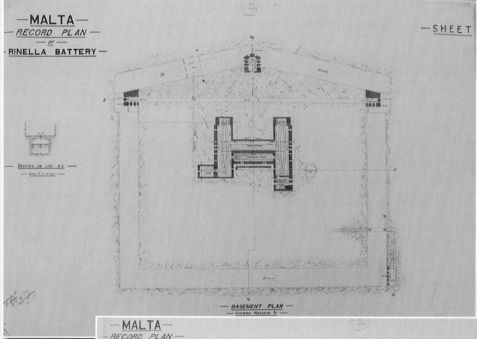

Plan showing underground features; the loading chambers, shifting lobby, lamp passages, lift shafts, and ammunition stores. Also shown are the caponiers and counterscarp gallery and the galleries leading to them

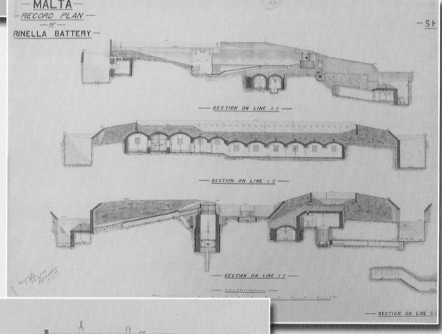

Sections showing (upper) through the ditch, barrack rooms, quadrangle, gun emplacement, and north caponier; (middle) through barrack rooms, entrance and guardroom; and (lower) through west demi-caponier, rammer shaft, lift shaft, gun emplacement, loading chamber no.1, pump room, engine room, and musketry parapet on roof

Section showing entrance and the Guthrie bridge spanning the ditch

Lord Sir John Lintorn Simmons KCB, Inspector General of Fortifications 1821-1903

Raised inscription above entrance of Rinella Battery marking year of emplacement of the 100 ton gun

Plan showing arcs of fire of coast artillery guns in main forts and batteries in the early 1880s. Note the sweeping arcs of the two 100-ton gun batteries on either side of the Grand Harbour.

an electric priming tube. In the latter case electrical current would be used to fire the gun.

New 100-ton gun batteries for Malta and Gibraltar

In 1877, the Inspector General of Fortifications, Sir John Lintorn Simmons was sent out to the Mediterranean by the War Office to report on the state of preparedness of the coastal defences of Malta and Gibraltar in view of the recent developments in the field of ship design and ordnance manufacture. Both stations were heavily fortified and well provided with ordnance. But the largest guns emplaced were those of just 38 tons, firing a 12.5-inch shell to a range of 6,000 yards. These guns could pierce 11.7 inches of wrought-iron armour within that range, and were thus no match for the new

Italian ships. Theoretically, the Italian navy had the potential of destroying any of the coastal defences at the two stations without being exposed to any serious danger.

On examining the situation, Simmons concluded that the two stations were to be rendered comfortably safe from the threat posed by any ships of the *Duilio* class only if similar guns as those on board the ships could be mounted on land. He thus suggested that four 100-ton guns were to be sent to Malta and to Gibraltar. Lintorn-Simmons' recommendations, prompted the Secretary of State for War to obtain from Sir W. G. Armstrong and Co. four 100-ton guns, two for each station.

The choice of location for these guns was left in the hands of the local authorities. For this reason a committee was formed under the chairmanship of H.E. the Governor and General Officer Commanding C.T. van Straubenzee, assisted by the Superintendent of HM Dockyard, Rear-Admiral, W.G. Luard. In all, some five sites on either side of the Grand Harbour were considered. These included Forts St Elmo, Ricasoli, and Tignè. But, owing to the sheer size of the gun in question and the cumbersome ancillary mechanical machinery, it was thought better to have the two guns accommodated separately in new works

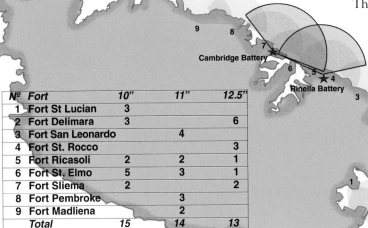

Nº	Fort	10"	11"	12.5"
1	Fort St Lucian	3		
2	Fort Delimara			6
3	Fort San Leonardo		4	
4	Fort St. Rocco			3
5	Fort Ricasoli	2	2	1
6	Fort St. Elmo	5	3	1
7	Fort Sliema	2		2
8	Fort Pembroke		3	
9	Fort Madliena		2	
	Total	15	14	13

General view of the
100-ton gun at
Rinella Gun Battery

built on both sides of the harbour. The two sites chosen where between Forts Tignè and Sliema on the Sliema side and between Forts Ricasoli and St Rocco on the Cottonera side.

The new locations afforded adequate protection to the entrance of the harbour for some 3 miles on either side. The arc of fire of both guns interlocked at the centre to provide double protection in case of an attempted forced entry by an enemy into the harbour.

Authorization for the commencement of two new 100-ton gun batteries was obtained from the War Office on 28 August 1878. The two new batteries were named Cambridge and Rinella respectively. The name 'Cambridge' was given in honour of HRH The Duke of Cambridge who visited the site while in Malta in 1878. Rinella battery took the name of the same land upon which it was built. At Gibraltar, the two 100-ton gun batteries were named after Queen Victoria and the governor of the time, Lord Napier of Magdala.

Description of batteries

In Malta two fully-fledged forts capable of providing their own defence were built. These took the shape of polygonal works built low into the ground to afford the best of protection against bombardment. Each was provided with a rolling bridge that spanned an all round dry ditch as protection against infantry attack. The ditch itself was provided with three caponiers and a counter-scarp gallery that could be reached from inside the fort. Each of these

A daily chore for the garrison – pumping of water from underground reservoir to the roof tanks

View of recently restored gorge wall and dry ditch

Reconstruction, showing manual lifting method of shells using a Weston differential pulley to place on loading trolley

Right: Excavations showing original positions of hydraulic accumulator, steam engine and boiler

had a number of loopholes through which the defenders could fire against anyone scaling down into the ditch. There was only one point of entry into these batteries, through a heavily armoured gate provided with loopholes. The gate itself was protected against long-range artillery fire by a bent-entry carved into the ground. A glacis or killing ground devoid of any thick or high vegetation was provided around each of these works to make it possible to control any movements around them.

Both batteries were provided with bomb-proof accommodation for their 35 man strong garrison. These barrack rooms ran along the back of the façade or gorge wall, thus doubling as a musketry gallery from where the fort could be defended through the windows. Further defence arrangements were also provided at roof level where a near continuous musketry parapet was provided.

The gun was positioned at the heart of the battery in a sunken emplacement to afford it protection against shelling. All ammunition was stored underneath the gun in two separate magazines, one for shells and another for gunpowder cartridges. On either side of the magazines, two loading chambers were provided, each

equipped with a hydraulically-operated ammunition lifts that led straight up to the gun floor. Each of the lift shafts led into a heavily-armoured turret with just one little port from where the ammunition was served into the gun. Two loading chambers and lifts were required to maintain an efficient rate of fire by alternating the loading process.

The 100-ton gun was powered by a steam-driven hydraulic set-up that was accommodated in a casemated engine room at ground level. Next to this room, a row of four manual pumps were provided to double up for the engine in case of it stopping. In line with these two rooms, but positioned on the extreme left of the gun, was the artillery store. This store served as

a point of entry for new ammunition, as a workshop and as a point of storage for mechanical parts and equipment. This room along with the engine and pump rooms formed the left and right flanks of the emplacement respectively.

The accommodation at the back of the battery comprised a guardroom, cookhouse, ablutions, and latrines along with nine barrack rooms. This block was separated from the gun emplacement and its underlying chambers by an open courtyard.

The battery was completed in 1886 at a cost of £15,047, which was somewhat less than what it had been initially projected to cost. Stone for building this battery was quarried on site while excavating the ditch. Yet,

Reconstruction of musketry fire through loopholes provided in the front gate

Reconstruction of musketry engagement in counter-scarp gallery

the front part was formed in thick monolithic concrete.

At Gibraltar only the front part of these batteries were required. All four batteries were built to a common plan. But Cambridge Battery was, for some obscure reason, built as a mirror image to all other three.

Lt. Col. Thomas Inglis

Transporting the gun

Disembarking of 100-ton gun at Sommerset Dock at HM Dockyard, Malta, 1882

Transporting the 100-ton guns from England to Gibraltar and Malta represented a huge undertaking for the military authorities. At first they contemplated to move the guns in the same way as Cleopatra's Needle had been transported to Britain from Egypt – sealed in an iron tube and

towed by a ship. But this option though practical was considered as too risky. For there always was the possibility that the floating tube would cast itself loose as had in fact happened in the case of the Egyptian obelisk when it went lost for weeks, only to be reclaimed back in calm waters by a passing ship!

After much deliberation, a decision was taken to transport these guns using the War Department Steam Ship *Stanley* which had to have its hold cleared as much as possible to make room for the big guns. The entire operation for moving and mounting the guns was entrusted in the capable hands of Lt. Col. (later Major-General) Thomas Inglis, RE Inglis was himself a military engineer of high repute with a keen interest in iron fortifications and mechanical engineering. He spent most of his time designing forts and improving artillery at the Royal Arsenal in Woolwich. On successfully completing the transportation and mounting of the 100-ton guns at Gibraltar and Malta, he was made a Commander of the Bath by Queen Victoria.

The War Department trasport vessel SS *Stanley* was to carry one gun at a time. The first of these left Woolwich on 22 August 1882. The voyage took 20 days to complete and, on 10

Transporting the 100-ton gun

Mr Dangerfield, haulage expert from Woolwich Arsenal who supervised the lifting operations

Mounting of the 100-ton gun

September 1882, the gun designated for Rinella Battery, arrived safely in the Grand Harbour.

In the meantime, great preparations were afoot in Malta, awaiting its arrival. A set of giant sheers was erected at Somerset Dock, in the Dockyard, to disembark the gun from the *Stanley*. A dockyard craft had to be specially modified to ferry it from the dockyard to Rinella Bay, from where it was to be transported to the battery. A temporary quay was also built at Rinella Bay where the gun was to be landed. The bay itself was deepened using underwater explosives, and the uphill road leading to Rinella Battery was widened and repaired in preparation for the impending transport operation.

In late 1883, while the front part of the battery was nearing its completion, the operation of transporting the gun to the battery was finally started. The gun was then loaded on a barge at the Dockyard and ferried across the harbour to Rinella Bay. On reaching its destination, it was unloaded using a set of heavy wooden sheers, and placed on a wooden sleigh running on metal rollers. An artillery company of 100 men, from 1 Battery 1 Brigade Scottish Division RA, was impressed to pull the gun barrel all the way up to the battery, using capstans, rollers, hydraulic jacks, and sheer muscle power!

Unsurprisingly, this task proved to be a long and arduous one indeed. It may suffice to say that it took 87 days to complete, most of which were taken to cover the 300 odd yards from

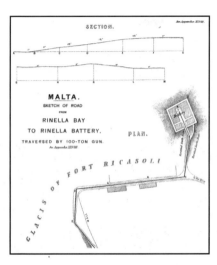

Plan taken from official WD report on transportation and mounting of the 100-ton guns showing route covered from landing place in Rinella Bay up to Rinella Battery.

21

Major D.D.T. O'Callaghan, RA

Captain G.S. Clarke, RE

Re-enactment activity by volunteers reconstructing daily life of the garrison

Rinella Bay to the battery. At 3 o'clock in the afternoon of 12 January 1884, with the help of a massive gantry erected temporarily over the gun emplacement, the gun barrel was lifted free from the sleigh and mounted on its traversing carriage that had already been set-up. With the gun in its place, Rinella Battery was handed over by the sappers to the gunners, in whose charge it remained for the next 22 years.

Service life

Work on this battery went on for another two years till it was finished in 1886. In March of that year, two officers from the Royal Artillery and Royal Engineers Works Committee were sent from Britain to inspect all 100-ton gun batteries in Gibraltar and Malta. The purpose of their mission was to ascertain that they were built as planned and that the guns and their machinery were working well. The two officers were Major D.D.T.

O'Callaghan, RA and Capt. G.S. Clarke, RE.

Following their inspection, O'Callaghan and Clarke presented a report about the state of all the batteries, faults found, and a list of recommendations to act upon. Both officers agreed that all was generally well at these batteries, although minor adjustments were required. Their suggestions included an increase in water supply for the operation of hydraulics in Malta and the provision of wash-out apparatus necessary to render the gun barrel safe after each round. They also recommended that the storage capacity of 33 shells was to be increased to 100, for which the shell pit was to be deepened in order to allow more shells to be stored in it.

Minor modifications were also recommended to the building of the battery itself, mainly by reducing the length of the two stone revetments on each side of the emplacement and the covering up of two musketry pits formed in the crests of the slopes on either side of the gun emplacement.

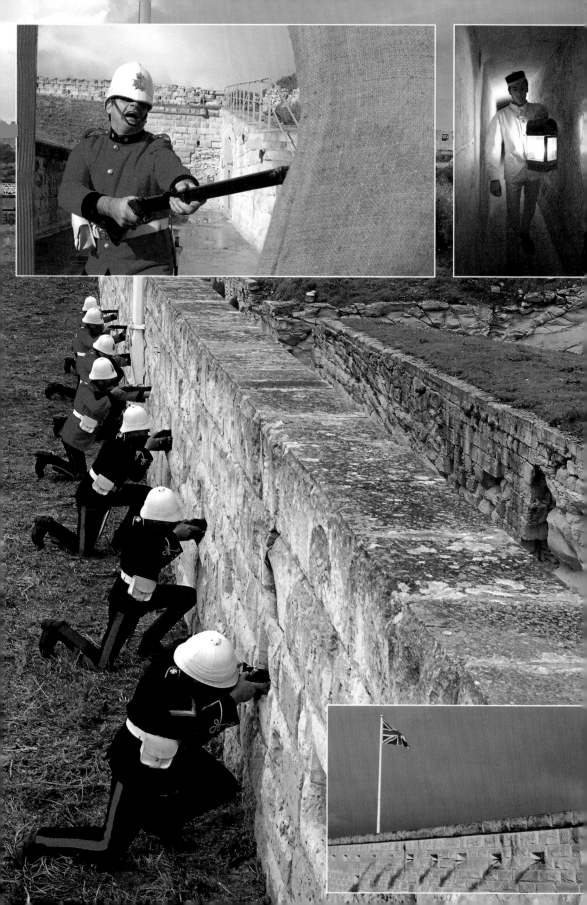

The garrison

The sheer size of the 100-ton gun required that the garrisons of these batteries be formed exclusively of specially trained men.

Each battery would be manned by a troop of 35 men drawn from the Royal Garrison Artillery. The duties of these men were chiefly centred on the working and firing of the gun. For that purpose, all men were uniquely issued with white duck uniforms for regular use.

A good part of this strength was taken up to form two loading crews for the distribution of the heavy ammunition from the stores onto loading trolleys down in the magazines. A smaller number would be employed in taking range; another two men would tend the steam boiler and the engine room. One man, termed 'the lamp man' was responsible for servicing lanterns, which were kept in little lighting windows in the wall, and thus keep the loading chambers and magazines lit up. A senior rank would occupy the traversing recess securely tucked within the huge concrete mass of the gun parapet from where the gun and all its machinery was operated by means of hydraulic controls. In case of alarm, a full company of infantrymen, 100 in all, was deemed necessary to defend the fort.

Army pay was one shilling a day. From this pay various stoppages were made to cover the ex-penses of cleaning materials, additional food condiments, regi-mental fund etc. leaving nearly nothing out of an already miserable wage.

The uniforms

From top:

Royal Malta Artillery (c. 1890)
Driver and Ceremonial Dress

Royal Malta Regiment of Militia (c. 1890)
Field Service and Review Orders

Royal Malta Artillery (c. 1890)
Khaki Field Service Order and Drummer

Royal Garrison Artillery (c. 1890)
Shirt Sleeve and Fatigue Orders

On opposite page:
Top left: Victorian soldier at bayonet practice
Top right: Lamp man in lighting passage
Main picture: Victorian soldiers manning the musketry parapet
Bottom left: Rifle fire through the Musketry Parapet

They thought that the revetment walls were effectively shell-traps around the emplacements. As for the pits, they considered these as superfluous and that they dangerously exposed the underlying engine room and artillery store to penetration by incoming enemy shells.

By the end of 1886, most of the recommendations made by O'Callaghan and Clarke on the 100-ton gun batteries, had been implemented, and the guns and their machinery were reported to be in full working order. Rinella Battery remained in service till 1906 during which period it saw no action. This was due to the fact that Malta was neither attacked nor was it directly involved in any conflict during that time.

Being just a small coastal battery, Rinella did not have a full garrison all the time. Rather, a small contingent of some seven men under the charge of a junior non-commissioned officer would be stationed on a regular basis.

"Will bark no more", 1910

The 100-ton as an a object of curiosity following its demise

Firing of 100-ton gun at Napier of Magdala Battery in Gibraltar

These acted as a caretaker guard, keeping the battery, its gun, and the machinery in the highest state of preparedness.

Occasionally, the 100-ton gun was fired on practice days. This gun was expected to last up to about 120 rounds, after which its bore would have been eroded to such an extent that its range and accuracy would be impaired. This can be best understood if one considers the immense size of the shell it fired and also the massive quantity of black powder that was required to propel such ordnance. Technically the gun could be re-tubed, that is having its internal barrel liner replaced, but that would have required the monster piece to be shipped back to Armstrong's for that operation, which for various reasons was very unlikely to happen.

On their part, the military took measures to lengthen as far as possible the service life of this gun, mainly by restricting its firing to not more than four rounds a year. But fear of eroding, the piece was not the only reason for this restriction. There was also the phenomenal cost involved for each firing which pressed the authorities to

exercise caution in peacetime. Each round fired from the 100-ton gun cost £100 – the equivalent of the salary of 2,400 soldiers for a day!

As one would expect, the firing of one of these guns elicited much attention from the civil population which is recorded to have congregated in great numbers on vantage points near the batteries to follow the unusual spectacle. Prior to each practice, the military would notify the public through the newspapers. This was done to forewarn those living in the vicinity of these forts to leave open their windows to limit any damage that the fierce shock created by these guns could cause. In addition, the local policeman was required to check that these apertures were left open in an effort to limit any possible complications later.

A good indication of what these gun firings were like can be glimpsed from a contemporary experience left to us by Henry M. Field, an American traveller who wrote, while in Gibraltar in 1889:

The guns had recently been tried, and found to be perfect, though the explosion was not so terrible as had at first been

Frontispiece of the report on 100-ton guns by O'Callaghan and Clarke

27

Modern reconstruction of military visual signalling at Rinella Battery

feared. There had been some apprehension that a weapon, which was to be so destructive to enemies, might not be an innocent toy to those who figured it; that it might split the ear-drums of gunners themselves. One who was present at the firing of one of the hundred ton guns told me that all who stood round expected to be deafened by the concussion. Yet when it came, they looked at each other with a mixture of surprise and disappointment. The sound was not in proportion to the size. Indeed our Consul tells me that some of the sixty-eight pounders are as ear-splitting as the hundred ton guns. But an English gentleman whom I met at Naples gave me a different report of his experience. He had just come from Malta, where they have a hundred ton gun mounted on the ramparts. One day, while at dinner at the hotel, they heard a crash, at which they all started from their seats, and rushed to the windows to throw them open, lest a second discharge should not leave a pane of glass unbroken. When about three miles at the sea they saw the splash, which was followed by a boom such as they never heard before. It was the most awful thunder rolling over the deep in billows, like waves of the sea, filling the whole horizon with the vast tremendous sound. It was 'the voice of God on the waters'.

Opposite page: Victorian infantry defending through the armoured gate

Aerial view of gun emplacement

Demise

The 100-ton gun was in many ways a white elephant. For already by the time that it was emplaced a significant development in the field of gunpowder and for that in artillery had rendered it entirely obsolete.

In the early 1880s, Sir Frederick Abel and Captain Andrew Nobel perfected cordite for artillery use. This new propellant, when ignited, burnt at a much slower rate than black powder. For that reason, it could not be safely used in muzzle-loading artillery where barrels were kept short due to the many problems posed by their loading. New and longer barrelled guns were needed for the new gunpowder for which the breech-loading gun proved to be an excellent candidate. Following early experimentation, it soon showed that this was to be the gun of the future and already in 1886, the first types of breech loading armament for naval and coastal defence use were being made. By the mid-1890s, muzzle-loading technology was completely superseded and gradually all such armament was replaced.

Despite these changes, the 100-ton gun was retained in front line service till 5 May 1905 when it was fired for the last time. In October of the following year, all 100-ton guns were reported as stripped and abandoned.

Aerial view of gun emplacement

Damage from aerial bombardment from the Second World War still visible today

Although all steam and hydraulic machinery was removed from the battery at this time, the 100-ton gun was left in its place.

After this date, the battery remained in some form of military use, mainly serving as a position finding station for artillery range taking in conjunction with nearby Fort Ricasoli, as Position Finding Station No. VII. This role seems to have ended by the mid-1930s when the battery passed under admiralty responsibility. At the time, the authorities feared a confrontation with Italy over the invasion of Abyssinia in 1935. Given the proximity of the island to Sicily, and the fact that Britain as a member of the League of Nations had imposed sanctions against Italy, the naval and military

authorities took precautions against the eventuality of Italian aerial strikes against the island. One such measure was the dispersal of all previously concentrated warlike stores to small bomb-proof buildings like Rinella Battery. Needless to say Rinella with its heavy vaulted construction fitted this role perfectly. But there was to be no war with Italy for another five years.

During the Second World War, other uses were found for Rinella Battery other than just a store. Its elevated roof served as an ideal Coast Watching Post for the 2nd Battalion Cheshire Regiment, whilst its rock-hewn galleries leading to its ditch defences were turned into air raid shelters mainly for the use of the immediate farming community.

Although of no more defensive use, Rinella Battery was hit several times during air raids. Significant damage from this period can still be viewed

Captain Andrew Nobel, manager of the Ordnance Factory at Elswick and co-inventor of the new slow burning gunpowder

The new 6-inch breech-loading gun produced by Elswick Ordnance Works in 1886

Right: Joint inspecting team from the War Department and private scrap merchants inspecting the 100-ton gun at Cambridge Battery, Sliema, prior to its cutting up in 1956

Below: Various views of the cutting up operation of the 100-ton gun at Cambridge Battery

along its left flank. Also, its glacis is still pock-marked with wartime bomb craters. Fortunately, its sturdy construction held on and no serious damage was received.

Salvage and preservation

In 1952 Britain made away with heavy coast and anti-aircraft artillery

in favour of modern missiles. In line with this, Malta Garrison HQ ordered the removal and scrapping of all old and unnecessary ordnance in forts. Hundreds of guns ancient and modern, some of which had rested in our forts since their time of building, were thus lost. Both 100-ton guns in Malta were earmarked for scrap. But fortunately only that at Cambridge Battery was removed. The saving of the Rinella gun is attributed to the fact that at the time the battery was still under the responsibility of the Admiralty, where the army order had no effect!

Military ownership of the battery ceased in 1965, as part of a mass surrender of property by the Ministry of Defence to the Government of Malta. For a brief period, it formed part of the new premises of the fledgling movie industry in Malta, and was used as a set location for scenes in epic films like *Hell boats*, *Zeppelin*, and *Shout at the Devil*. Its last direct connection with the film industry was when part of the entrance was turned into a medieval blacksmith shop for the Italian film *Christopher Columbus*, which unfortunately proved to be one of the greatest blockbuster flops in cinema history.

In 1991, the government of Malta entrusted Rinella Battery to *Fondazzjoni Wirt Artna* – the Malta Heritage Trust with the aim of restoring it back to its former state and to turn it into a museum. Since then, innumerable hours of voluntary work have been spent in the pursuit of this ambition, the result of which can now hopefully be seen and enjoyed by all.

Re-enactment activities help the public to understand better the history and nature of the fort

Loading the 100-ton gun required the gun to be first turned mechanically to face any of the two loading turrets positioned on either of its flanks, depending on which one of them is ready to load. All ammunition would then be brought up to the gun floor level using hydraulic hoists on board a loading trolley. At that level an 18-metre long hydraulic rammer is activated to push the shell and cartridge home into the barrel of the gun. Following that, the gun is trained onto its target and fired. All this required just 6 minutes to complete.

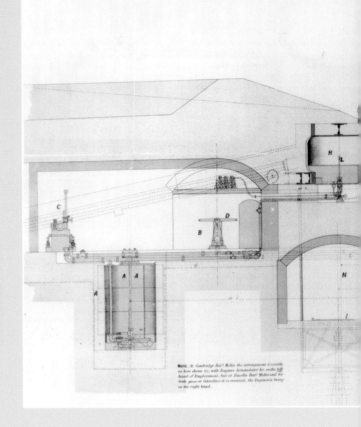

Gun Specifications

Type:	Rifled Muzzle Loader, Land Service	
Calibre:	450 mm	
Nominal weight of barrel:	103.64 tonnes	
Total length:	9.952 m	
Material:	Exterior	Wrought iron
	Interior	Toughened steel
Bore:	Calibre	450 mm
	Length	9.22 m
	Capacity	1602.4 L
Chamber:	Diameter	500 mm
	Length	1.517 m
	Capacity	279.4 L
Rifling:	System	Polygroove, plain section
	Twist	Increasing from 1 turn in 150 calibres at the breech to 1 turn in 50 calibres at 73.5 mm from the muzzle, remainder uniform, 1 in 50 calibre
	Grooves	Number 28
		Depth 3.2 mm
		Width 27.9 mm
		Length 7.693 m
Means of rotation:	Copper gas check	

Vent:	Axial with shutter
Chamber:	Cylindrical, terminated at each end by a frustum of a cone
Sights:	Two sets of reflecting sights, one on each side
Maker:	Sir W.G. Armstrong & Co., Newcastle upon Tyne
Year of make:	1878
Type of carriage:	Traversing slide and platform
Height of parapet:	2.44 m
Weight of carriage:	20.6797 tonnes
Weight of platform:	26.1505 tonnes
Inclination of platform:	4°
Arc of traversing:	180°
Maximum angle of elevation:	11°
Maximum angle of depression:	11°
Working power:	Combination of steam and hydraulic
Methods of firing:	Tube, vent sealing, electric by Leclanchè battery
	Tube, vent sealing, friction by lanyard
Weight of shell:	907 kg
Maximum range:	6,400 m
Penetration at maximum range:	0.4 m wrought iron armour
Weight of propelling charge:	204.1 black prismatic powder
Crew:	6 NCOs & 16 gunners
Number of grooves:	28
Means of rotation:	Copper gas check
Vent:	Axial

Glossary

Battery A work designed for a group of guns and their equipment, also artillery formation

Bomb-proof A structure that can withstand plunging shell fire

Bore The inside of a gun barrel

Breech The rear end of a gun

Bullet-proof Protection against the effect of small-arms fire

Calibre The diameter of the bore of a gun

Caponier A casemate which projects into the ditch of a fort, intended to provide flanking fire along it

Casemate Bomb-proof vaulted chamber within the ramparts providing an emplacement for a gun and/or a barrack room

Caseshot An ammunition round made up from a great amount of small projectiles sealed in a cylindrical container, designed to burst when fired from a gun. Normally used as an anti-personnel weapon or against small craft

Chase The over-all length of a gun barrel between the trunnions and its muzzle

Counter-scarp Exterior slope of a ditch

Counterscarp Gallery A chamber built into the counterscarp of a fort to mount weapons for firing as flank defence or as a place to start countermining

Ditch Deep excavation around a fort to serve as an effective obstacle against an attack from land

Drop-ditch An additional ditch within the main ditch of a fort placed in front or around ditch defence structures

En Barbette A battery position where the protective parapet is low enough for the gun to fire over it without the need for an embrasure

Enfilade To fire at right angles to the inside or outside of a fort's wall, killing men with flanking fire against which they have no protection

Flank The lateral extremes of a work

Glacis A mass of earth raised on the outer side of the ditch to protect the scarp wall from distant breaching fire. It affords no cover to an enemy from fire of the parapet

Gorge Rear, whether opened or closed, of any work

Guthrie bridge Type of rolling bridge named after C.T. Guthrie, Scottish engineer in the 1860s

Loophole An aperture in a wall for firing a rifle through

Magazine A place for the safe storage of gun powder

Musketry The use of small arms

Muzzle The front-end of a gun barrel

Muzzle-loader Any gun loaded from its (muzzle-end) front

Parapet A bank or wall for the protection of soldiers on the rampart, over or through which guns fire

Rifled Breech Loader (R.B.L.) A gun whose bore was cut along its axis with spiral grooves, and is loaded from its back

Rifled Muzzle Loader (R.M.L.) Type of artillary having a rifled bore and loaded from the front

Scarp The inner wall of a ditch, also the face of a work

Traversing platform Wooden or metal platform which supported a gun and its carriage and which could be traversed within a gun emplacement on racer trucks. Those used on racers were flanged on one or both edges

Trunnion A projection at the point of balance of a gun barrel, on which it swivels

Vent A touch-hole drilled into the body of a muzzle-loading barrel, in the cascabel area for igniting the charge

Work Technical term for any form of fortified position

On assignment

Most of the photography of this book, as well as those in the Insight Heritage Guides Series have been entrusted to Daniel Cilia. Heritage Books is proud to have acquired the services of such a photographer.

Daniel was born in Rabat, Gozo in 1963. He exhibited solo in 1986 at the National Museum of Fine Arts, Malta. That same year he was awarded the Licentiate of the Royal Photographic Society of Great Britain.

He has lectured at the National College of Art, Crafts and Design, in Oslo, Norway (1988) and directed the Photographic Department at the Art Institute of Florence from 1990 to 1995.

Cilia also held exhibitions in Malta, Italy, France, Germany, Belgium, the Czech Republic, Canada, Australia, and the USA.

His work has been published in several magazines in Europe, Japan, and the USA. Cilia's photographic studies on the island of Malta have appeared in the books such as:*Legacy in Stone* (1993), *Melit et Gaul* (1995),*Valletta* (1997), *Mdina* (1998), and *The Three Cities* (1998). In 1999, *The Temple of the Knights of Malta* (2000), *Malta: Influence and Patronage* (2001), *The Sovereign Palaces of Malta, Malta: Prehistory and Temples* (2002), *Malta, the Baroque Island* (2003) and *Malta before History* (2004).

The 100-ton gun batteries at Gibraltar

As in Malta, two 100-ton gun batteries were built in Gibraltar to secure the naval anchorage there. However, these were built devoid of any peacetime gun crew accommodation. Neither were they provided with any self-defensible capabilities. This was due to the restriction of space on the Rock and the fact that barrack accommodation was only a short distance away from both batteries. For their defence the two batteries relied on adjacent works forming part of the defensive enceinte.

The first of the two batteries built in Gibraltar was Victoria Battery in 1879. This was constructed at the end of the Grand Parade beyond Southport Gate. Four years later, Napier of Magdala Battery, named after the incumbent governor of Gibraltar was completed. This occupied a commanding position on the cliff above Rosia Bay. With its arc of fire at 180 degrees, it ran north over the landward defences of the New Mole and south along the coast towards Europa Point. Victoria Battery lay further to the north, a little way outside the South Front and on the Grand Parade. Its arc of fire at 180 degrees extended to the north and to Europa Point to the south. In this way these two guns covered the whole waters of Gibraltar Bay.

Today, only Napier of Magdala Battery is still complete with its gun and most of its original hydraulic equipment. Incidentally, the gun seen at that battery came from Victoria Battery. This was prompted in the late 1890s, as a result of the gun at Napier of Magdala cracking up during a double loading incident. It was felt at the time that the position of this battery was far superior to that of Victoria, and a barrel change was warranted. As the procurement of a new barrel from Elswick would take too long, it was decided that a barrel switch would take place from one battery to another. Victoria Battery was never used again, and only a small portion of it now survives as part of the Town Fire Station next to the beautiful Alameida botanical gardens.